GO!

10 Blessings That Follow When You Obey His Still Small Voice

YOLANDA PERRY

Yolanda Perry

Scripture taken from the Amplified Bible, Copyright © 1954, 1958, 1962, 1964, 1965, 1987 by The Lockman Foundation. Used by permission.

The Holy Bible, Berean Study Bible, BSB Copyright ©2016 by Bible Hub Used by Permission. All Rights Reserved Worldwide.

Scripture taken from the Contemporary English Version © 1991, 1992, 1995 by American Bible Society, Used by Permission.

Scripture quotations are from the ESV® Bible (The Holy Bible, English Standard Version®), copyright © 2001 by Crossway, a publishing ministry of Good News Publishers. Used by permission. All rights reserved.

Scriptures and additional materials quoted are from the Good News Bible © 1994 published by the Bible Societies/HarperCollins Publishers Ltd UK, Good News Bible© American Bible Society 1966, 1971, 1976, 1992. Used with permission.

GOD'S WORD is a copyrighted work of God's Word to the Nations. Quotations are used by permission. Copyright 1995 by God's Word to the Nations. All rights reserved.

Scripture quotations marked HCSB®, are taken from the Holman Christian Standard Bible®, Copyright © 1999, 2000, 2002, 2003, 2009 by Holman Bible Publishers. Used by permission. HCSB® is a federally registered trademark of Holman Bible Publishers.

Scriptures marked KJV are taken from the KING JAMES VERSION (KJV): KING JAMES VERSION, public domain.

Scripture quotations marked MSG are taken from *THE MESSAGE*, copyright © 1993, 1994, 1995, 1996, 2000, 2001, 2002 by Eugene H. Peterson. Used by permission of NavPress. All rights reserved. Represented by Tyndale House Publishers, Inc.

Scripture quotations taken from the New American Standard Bible® (NASB), Copyright © 1960, 1962, 1963, 1968, 1971, 1972, 1973, 1975, 1977, 1995 by The Lockman Foundation Used by permission. www.Lockman.org

Scriptures taken from the Holy Bible, New International Version®, NIV®. Copyright © 1973, 1978, 1984, 2011 by Biblica, Inc.™ Used by permission of Zondervan. All rights reserved worldwide. www.zondervan.com The "NIV" and "New International Version" are trademarks registered in the United States Patent and Trademark Office by Biblica, Inc.™

NKJV. Scripture taken from the New King James Version®. Copyright © 1982 by Thomas Nelson. Used by permission. All rights reserved.

Scripture quotations are taken from the Holy Bible, New Living Translation, copyright ©1996, 2004, 2007, 2013, 2015 by Tyndale House Foundation. Used by permission of Tyndale House Publishers, Inc., Carol Stream, Illinois 60188. All rights reserved.

Scriptures marked TLB are taken from the THE LIVING BIBLE (TLB): Scripture taken from THE LIVING BIBLE copyright© 1971. Used by permission of Tyndale House Publishers, Inc., Carol Stream, Illinois 60188. All rights reserved.

GO! 10 Blessings That Follow When You Obey His Still Small Voice
Copyright © 2017 by Yolanda Perry
www.speak2myheart.org

ISBN-13: 978-1979077187
ISBN-10: 1979077185

Printed in the United States of America. All rights reserved under International Copyright Law. Contents and/or cover may not be reproduced in whole or in part in any form without the expressed written consent of the author.

Yolanda Perry

DEDICATION

To Apostles Ryan & Joy LeStrange
For every word spoken over me
For every prayer prayed for me
For every impartation made to me
For every example you have shown me

CONTENTS

DEDICATION v
ACKNOWLEDGMENTS ix
PROLOGUE 1
INTRODUCTION 9
BLESSING #1 RELATIONAL UPGRADE 23
BLESSING #2 TURNING THE TABLES 37
BLESSING #3 ALL IN THE FAMILY 51
BLESSING #4 POSITIONED FOR PROMOTION 63
BLESSING #5 FINANCIAL FLOODGATES OPEN 75
BLESSING #6 CALL-IN CONVERSION CLAIMS 87
BLESSING #7 BOOMERANG BLESSINGS 95
BLESSING #8 ACCESS TO A FAVOR FEST 103
BLESSING #9 DIVINE PROTECTION 113
BLESSING #10 ONE OF THEM 129
CONCLUSION 139
EPILOGUE 143
BIBLE VERSION KEY 147
ABOUT THE AUTHOR 149

ACKNOWLEDGMENTS

Darius, Kadazia and Kyra. I am still amazed God has entrusted me with such treasures, to shape each of your lives into what He designed it to be. When I laid in ICU unconscious for five days, you each thrusted into purpose in a way that still astounds me today. Thank you for guarding my life with such care. Thanks for understanding and cheering me on each time I had to *GO*!

Apostles Ryan LeStrange, Jennifer LeClaire and Joe Joe Dawson. I showed up at Elijah's Altar in Loganville, GA January 2016 with just a word from the Lord that I had to get there. The prophetic words you each spoke over my life still burn within me today. You all have so much to do with this charge to write *GO*!

Donna Partow. When you prophesied 2017 would be my BREAK OUT year, I knew it to be the word of the Lord. Thank you for showing me exactly what the benefits are when we lay at His feet with no agenda at all…and how to execute when He comes up with one for us!

Tasha Springer. I proudly call you my spiritual daughter. Thank you for praying me through from the moment God gave me this assignment, just an outline scratched out on a piece of paper. And thank you for leading my Keep Me Covered Crew!

Yolanda Perry

PROLOGUE

Then He said, "Go out, and stand on the mountain before the LORD." And behold, the LORD passed by, and a great and strong wind tore into the mountains and broke the rocks in pieces before the LORD, but the LORD was not in the wind; and after the wind an earthquake, but the LORD was not in the earthquake; and after the earthquake a fire, but the Lord was not in the fire; and after the fire a still small voice.

1 Kings 19:11-12 (NKJV)

There is oftentimes this misconception that God only speaks in the roar of a voice, as though baritone is His only tempo. However, the truth is God speaks in many ways—dreams and visions; impressions; circumstances;

prophetic utterances through people; and more. One way in particular is through a still small voice as mentioned in Scripture. When God speaks in this way, we must be in a place of stillness, and openness, to hear exactly what it is He is trying to say to us. Otherwise, we are likely to miss it. And one thing I have learned about missing God's season concerning a matter is the waiting season for it to come back around can be pretty gruesome. I call it missing a Kairos moment—that now moment to move or take action with God's wind of grace to do so.

While completely engrossed in another writing project, which was originally due to be released this summer, 2017, I waited with anticipation for the promised Facebook Live dedicated to launch the scribes, with Apostles Ryan LeStrange and Jennifer LeClaire. There had been a previous announcement that it was coming; and I was excited about what would be shared that would encourage me with the book I already had underway. Wow! It was worth the wait. They certainly delivered. It was so encouraging, so uplifting and so invigorating. I was eager for what was promised to come as they declared the word of the Lord, that this is the time for many to launch into their writing careers. I thought, "Oh God, this is it. I am on track with the book I am currently writing. Can summer be tomorrow already so I can release this now?" I am five chapters into this manuscript and completely on track with my goal and the time set to publish it. Everything they shared that day was so profound and such great confirmation for me...UNTIL...

Apostle Ryan LeStrange began to declare more of what God was saying to the scribes that day. He prophesied full books would be written in the month of March.

Hold up...wait a minute!

I needed to check the calendar because I was quite certain this was being said in real time...in March. As a matter of fact, at the time of the live broadcast, it was two weeks into the month, to be exact.

Whole books written? Did he really just say that?

Well, I have learned to never question a word from the Lord. Not to mention I could feel the wind of God, even coming through the airwaves, on what was being released as prophetic utterances. However, I did passively praise God for whomever He would use to produce a book in such a short amount of time. I had heard of people doing this, but not people like me. When would I have time to do that? It was taking everything out of me to keep the goal I had set for a few months away. So I dismissed the notion that this word was for me at the time. I needed to keep my head on straight, as I was already in full swing with the assignment that was (and still is) before me. About a week passed by and a slight nudging and reminder of the word came, but nothing that gave me any witness that I should attempt to write a book…this month.

Then suddenly one morning in prayer it hit me...I heard the word *GO* in my spirit. It did not necessarily come with force. In all honesty, it was more of a still small voice experience as previously described. At that moment, I had no context at all but knew there was more and began to lean and press into God about this word, *GO*. As I did, He began to breathe upon that one-little-two-letter-word. I somehow knew at that moment, it was a book, and I would be its author. Yes I would be God's scribe for this message. Yes...I had to write it...in March. Although that meant this would need to happen in exactly seven days to fulfill the word that had already been spoken, I flat out refused to believe anything other than the fact that God could and would do this through me. It was more of a matter of whether I was going to respond to His charge to do it...to write it...to *GO*.

Now let me put all of the factors—personal challenges and limitations—into perspective here. At the time, I responded to the instruction, here is a list of the very real circumstances I was facing:

1. I work full time. To add, at this very moment, I am under not-so-friendly fire at my place of employment. My character has been assassinated and my integrity has been called into question. In one week, I was called into my supervisor's office twice to undergo the most humiliating interrogation, being asked, what I consider to be the most ridiculous line of questions, which insinuated I cannot be trusted. Thank God for His vindication in the matter; but still going through it was completely exhausting.

2. I am a single mom, and currently have two bonus girls in tow through foster care. One particular case requires constant, daily communication to get things done in school in hopes to pass the current classes. Not to mention the homework shuffle and check-ins to make sure everything is done and ready

to be presented to the teachers each day as we near the end of this grading period.

3. One day into the writing process, I fell ill with whatever nasty viral infection my children left behind when they decided to hang out in my bed the week before while they were sick.

I could certainly go on and on; but surely you can get a pretty clear picture. I had a choice to make: consider my circumstances or embrace the word of the Lord. My obedience to His still small voice has resulted in what you get to dive into at this very moment—the finished product. Since March, some things shifted a bit. But the book was produced nonetheless. Enjoy the journey as you travel with me through *GO! 10 Blessings That Follow When You Obey His Still Small Voice.*

Yolanda Perry

INTRODUCTION

Sometimes what seems to be the simplest of instructions could be loaded with all sorts of possibilities as well as uncertainties. You may sense it, yet not really even know the fullness of what you are hearing God speak at a given time. You may even question what He says really means, in those moments. Nonetheless, in each instance, you are always faced with a decision to make: to obey or to not obey. Those two options are simple in and of themselves when you think about it. Or are they? I would argue that each of them can be considered a bit complex—complicated even. The God kind of complicated, that is. It does not matter which you choose to do, it will cost you greatly. When the moment of truth arises, you just have to decide, "What am I willing to pay?" Whether your ultimate response is to obey or disobey, there will always be consequences that will follow. History has proven to me that obedience oftentimes means navigating through some of the roughest and toughest terrain. However, it will always yield the most desirable results in the end.

> *Jesus commented, "Even more blessed are those who hear God's Word and guard it with their lives!"*
>
> **Luke 11:28 (MSG)**

Wait. What? To obey God's word means to guard and keep watch over it? That sounds pretty labor-intensive to me. I wonder if I get to add that to my resume? Maybe; maybe not. But even if not, the promise to be blessed is enough for me to steward well every word God entrusts to me.

Over the course of my life as a Christian, much of my journey has been about learning to hear, know and respond to the voice of God. Much of what God has asked of me over the years have seemed a bit far-fetched, out-of-the-box, and sometimes even down right crazy—too nonsensical to even mention to others at times. Yet each time I knew what I was hearing and was determined to obey Him no matter what.

Why?

Because in every case God instructed me to do something, He always proved His plan was far greater than my thought process could ever prove to be. So I always went along for the ride, whether smooth or turbulent, even if I was a little reluctant at times.

In this book, we will explore what I consider to be one of God's signature expressions when it comes to Him giving instructions: *GO*. Just by doing a casual internet search of the word, *GO*, I discovered it means, "to move from one place or point to another, travel." Oh how I love to travel. That word alone has the potential to take me on a rabbit trail. Yet I will contain myself and focus here on the journey set before us. This book covers ten blessings available to us when we walk in obedience to the Father. Throughout I include personal testimonies as examples of each of those blessings and to demonstrate God's faithfulness. So, let's *GO*. No pun intended.

Whenever God gives instructions, it usually will require movement, of some form, on your part. It will likely challenge and provoke you to take action that will call for you to make adjustments, shift focuses, or even shake things up in your world altogether. Nevertheless, obedience to whatever the instruction is will unlock the door to the blessings God has waiting for you on the other side of *GO*.

As I continued exploring, I was even more captivated by the synonyms listed for the word GO:

Move.
Proceed.
Make one's way.
Advance.
Progress.
Pass.

Each of these words is a call to action, just like Abram originally received from God when

He instructed him to *GO*…from one place to another. At the time, God did not give him elaborate instructions, only told him He wanted him to leave one place and go to another; and assured him he would be blessed for his obedience.

> *GOD told Abram: "[GO] Leave your country, your family, and your father's home for a land that I will show you. I'll make you a great nation and bless you. I'll make you famous; you'll be a blessing. I'll bless those who bless you; those who curse you I'll curse. All the families of the Earth will be blessed through you."So Abram left just as GOD said, and Lot left with him. Abram was seventy-five years old when he left Haran. Abram took his wife Sarai and his nephew Lot with him, along with all the possessions and people they had gotten in Haran, and set out for the land of Canaan and arrived safe and sound.*

Abram passed through the country as far as Shechem and the Oak of Moreh. At that time the Canaanites occupied the land. GOD appeared to Abram and said, "I will give this land to your children." Abram built an altar at the place GOD had appeared to him. He moved on from there to the hill country east of Bethel and pitched his tent between Bethel to the west and Ai to the east. He built an altar there and prayed to GOD.

Abram kept moving, steadily…

Genesis 12:1-9 (MSG)

Abram heeded God's word to him, which included a maybe not-so-simple instruction, which was laced with some heavy duty promises. To some, it may not seem like a big deal to be required to move. Yet I am reminded of many Permanent Changes of Station or PCS moves over the course of eleven years I was enlisted in the U.S. Army. At the start of my army career, other than having to leave my son behind for my mother to care for, it was pretty exciting packing up my bags and heading off for basic training at Fort Jackson, SC and then on to Fort Leonard Wood, MO. Even making the transition to Fort Drum, NY was pretty exhilarating. That is until I discovered I would not be anywhere close to the big cities where all the real happenings were. Nonetheless, I was quite content with receiving orders to *GO* from one place to another. However, that got pretty cumbersome rather quickly as I found myself on orders to move every year, except when I transferred to Germany and was there on a mandatory two year tour. I was exhausted, had eventually become a mother of two, married at the time, and then another baby. I was over the *GO* routine with the military. And in my case, I knew exactly where I would be going next, what my assignment would be, and had a unit in place to support me wherever I showed up.

Abram, on the other hand, had nothing except a word from the Lord; was in his old age; and had his wife, his nephew, and the group of people he took with him. Along the way, he had to convince them of what he, himself, was hearing and knew to be the voice of God speaking to him. In times like these, sometimes it is best to travel light, if you know what I mean. Thankfully in Abram's case, he knew the people of Haran whom he had chosen to take along with him. Imagine if he had a bunch of murmurers and complainers traveling with him as Moses did when he was leading the children of Israel out of Egypt. Even in the beginning, God's grace was surely sufficient for Abram (See 2 Corinthians 12:9). Not only grace, but also wisdom is a remarkable sustainer for sure. Imagine if he took all the backbiters, naysayers, secret sabotagers, and the like, along for this journey. The outcome, which we will discuss later, might look a whole lot different.

Without any sort of master plan, Abram gathered the necessities and set out to obey the Lord without hesitation. I read several different translations of this passage. Not one portrayed Abram as having any reluctance. He neither asked for more time nor a moment to process the instruction God had given him. He did not attempt to ponder his own thoughts of what this meant or where he might end up. He did not weigh out the pros and cons of what could possibly go right or potentially go all wrong. Nope.

He heard Him speak.

He knew God's voice.

He got to stepping.

Specifically, when God told Abram to *GO*, the Scripture says, "So Abram left just as God said…" As he proceeded to move, to *GO* forward, to make his way to wherever God might be leading him; God met Abram again in route for a little pep talk. Again, God began to describe some of the blessings He had in store for Abram for taking this leap of faith with Him. That is just the kind of God we serve. He understands we can get weary, especially if we wander aimlessly with instructions as abstract as the ones Abram received in the beginning. God began to encourage him by assuring

Abram this journey served a purpose far greater than himself. At the first checkpoint, God began to tell Abram of the blessings in store for his children as well. Once Abram advanced to new, unfamiliar territory, God told him He would give his offspring land that was occupied by the Canaanites at the time.

That was all Abram needed to keep going. He continued to progress and advance as God continued to reassure him. And the Scripture points out that *"Abram kept moving, steadily..."*, which is all God requires when He gives us a mandate. When God speaks a word, we must consider what could be hanging in the balance, what opportunity might be missed, or even how many souls may be lost if we choose not to respond with obedience. I can only imagine what might have happened if I responded favorably to every God-breathed instruction to *GO* the first time I heard each of them.

- How many lost souls would have found Jesus and discovered the Truth?

- What would ministry look like for me in this very moment?

- Where would I be in my career and ministry right now?

- How many would be healed at the laying on of my own hands?

- What influence would I have with those who could help build the Kingdom?

- What relationships would I have formed and established?

- Which nations would I have been welcomed to come and preach the Gospel in?

- Whose life might be spared because of the words I spoke to them?

I am shaking my head as I write that. I am challenged. I am moved. I am shaken. I am provoked. I am determined…to readjust my thinking, to move according to God's will and not my own. No longer will I listen passively;

but rather I will press in intently, that I may hear clearly what His still small voice has to say…and then endeavor to respond instantly every single time.

I am sensing so strongly that God wants to do the unthinkable, unimaginable for us. He wants to flex His abilities, and show us what we are entitled to when we simply obey Him. I, for one, do not want to forgo what He wants to do any longer. I want to experience the fullness of His goodness. I want to see His plan, purpose and perfect will manifest in my life and yours too. I want to see His wondrous works. Don't you?

> *Now to him who is able to do immeasurably more than all we ask or imagine, according to his power that is at work within us…*
>
> **Ephesians 3:20 (NIV)**

Normally, when this Scripture is read or quoted, much emphasis is made on what God can do. However, we ought not ignore the latter part of the verse, the condition that it is the power being active and alive in us that works in conjunction with God's ability "to do exceeding abundantly above all we ask or think" (as the King James Version puts it) on our behalf. I believe this is a NOW season for this to come to fruition. And there is a fresh wind on the *GO* mandate from God. I further believe we will begin to see instant results as we hearken unto His still small voice. Yes…I believe there will be an accelerated release of blessings for those who will move in His will, His purpose, and His timing.

May you even be pursued by His blessings as you *GO* forth in Him!

BLESSING #1
RELATIONAL UPGRADE

If you do what the LORD wants, he will make certain each step you take is sure.

Psalm 37:23 (CEV)

More often than not, the charge to *GO* will be a major inconvenience, seem completely untimely, require great financial sacrifice, and have the scent of presumptuousness. In short, what God is asking you to do in that moment will likely seem totally ridiculous to everyone around you, and probably to you too. Yet you sense within yourself an instant inner witness something like, "I have to *GO*". Whatever the instruction is in that time, it sets your knower into high alert…and you are convinced you have to follow through with the given assignment. That is all the seed needed in that moment. You suddenly become the designated steward of it. Your faith becomes its fertilizer. You must watch over it well in order to realize the fullness of its intended purpose. And sometimes that purpose just happens to be to discover key relationships God wants to bring into your life. A *GO*, when you hearken unto it, oftentimes will lead you into some of the most amazing divine connections and God-ordained relationships.

Even before I gave my heart to Christ, my steps were surely ordered by Him. When I went into the military, I had no idea what I was in for. Here is the craziest thing. Going in the military was not at all my idea in the first place. In high school, my older sister, Lisa, came up with this far-out idea that we should enlist in the army on the buddy system. That seemed like the thing to do back in the day. We would be guaranteed to go through training and be assigned at our first duty station together. Though going off to college was what I had in mind, I went along with her idea, as we both wanted a ticket out of where we are from, at that time. I do not remember seriously preparing to make this happen. I only remember when it was time to get moving on it, I found myself moving forward with recruiters for testing and physical examinations. The short of the story is the buddy plan turned into a solo side step of sorts, as my sister changed her mind. When Lisa decided not to enlist, I somehow felt like I still needed to *GO*. At the time I was not even serving God. Yet His handprint was all over my journey, my life.

I can remember as far back as my first duty station making friends with people in the barracks, who went to church even though they were not serving God. They partied all night on Saturday, but their upbringing compelled them to get to God's House every Sunday. They invited me along. I distinctly remember sitting in the first service I attended and being called out by the preacher. I was sitting way in the back. I can even remember the little red dress I was wearing (that I could only dream of fitting into today). I promise there is a moral of this story here.

As a result of following through with my thought that I should still *GO* into the military, despite the fact the original plans were altered, God allowed me to come into contact with the right people. There were hundreds in my unit; but I befriended the very ones who were assigned to get me to the House to get a prophetic word spoken over my life. There were hundreds in the congregation that day. I was sitting in the back of the church among my friends who had been attending the church long before I came to that duty station. None of them had had that experience before. Yet God used my connection to them to get to me the word He had for me. I do not remember the specifics of the prophecy, only that it was talking about my destiny in Christ. The experience of having God single me out in the crowd of hundreds was more of the matter for me. At first, I thought this was a normal occurrence until my friends assured me it was not. This sort of thing only happened occasionally, and apparently never to any of them. That made it all the more impactful for me. Ironically, over the years, this would happen to me in different conferences, events, etc., as a result of me following the unction to *GO* when God said so.

Just over a year ago, I received a charge to *GO* from God. He instructed me to attend a particular event. While traveling is my happy place, there were many factors I had to consider when God spoke this to me:

1. I had promised my daughter, Kyra, who was graduating high school that year that I would not add any more trips to my schedule until after she left for college. It was my desire to be present and an active part of her senior year, especially since she would be moving to another state to attend the college of her choice.

2. At the time, I sensed God nudging me to attend this said conference, Kyra was away on a service and study trip to Africa, with no way of being contacted. I could not share my dilemma with her and get her blessing to recant my commitment a little. And Kyra was not

set to return home until one week before this event.

3. I had already committed to another trip, a few months later, which Kyra had already approved of; and I really needed clarity from God about whether He was requiring me to cancel one for the other.

4. I could not afford a trip with such short notice, even if Kyra would say, "Yippy... *GO* do what God has called you to do Mom!"

You are probably wondering...How did all of this play out?

I had heard this conference announced a few times on social media. The theme, *Pressing Into the Prophetic Shift: A New Breed Revival Network (NBRN) Event* was so intriguing to say the least. Yet I never even considered attending due to the aforementioned reasons. Then suddenly, it all started with a strong impression I felt.

"You. Need. To. Get. There!" is what I sensed. I could not shake it.

It had only been a couple of months since I had stumbled upon the ministry of three Revivalists. Their words, backed by their passion for God, made a sound that resonated with what had been echoing on the inside of me for quite some time. It was as though something leaped within me, just like Elizabeth's encounter with Mary when they were both pregnant (See Luke 1:41).

First, Joe Joe Dawson's periscope was shared by someone I was following. When I listened to his teaching, it instantly spoke to a specific spiritual need. Second, this Joe Joe person mentioned the name, Jennifer LeClaire in his broadcast. I wrote it down and followed her later. In just a few days a notification came. Jennifer was sharing a very brief taping of a podcast. Yep…I instantly knew I needed to glean from her too. Third, about a week or so later…Jennifer was doing a broadcast of Ryan LeStrange preaching. The message, at that time, escapes me, as I have taken in so much more since then. Nonetheless, Ryan's passion for revival compelled me to find and follow his ministry as well.

At the time, I was in a rather peculiar place with regard to the prophetic calling on my life and really needed some advice and encouragement. Out of my comfort zone I stepped. I reached out to Joe Joe Dawson. Did I mention I knew nothing about this person? Of course I was surprised when he responded and was gracious enough to speak with me. In that initial conversation, I discovered he was serving alongside Jennifer and Ryan as part of NBRN. My first thought…"Now this is divine connection!" Disclosure: Today, I refer to these men and woman of God as Apostle, their true calling. However, I write this based on how I learned of them during that time…first name basis being all I had heard.

As impossible as attending the event seemed, there was no denying that God was wooing me to *GO*. I had to remind myself that He never disappoints when He tells me to do something. So, I put it before Him in this way,

"Absolutely I will *GO*, Lord, if You make the way." And He did!

What was my strategy?

> *Don't worry about anything; instead, pray about everything. Tell God what you need, and thank him for all he has done.*
>
> **Philippians 4:6 (NLT)**

Once I put it before God, I just expected Him to make it happen. I trusted His plan would manifest itself, as it always has for me. It did in a supernatural way. He was the one who gave me this nonsensical idea to travel across country at a moment's notice anyway. Yes…when He said *GO*, the conference was just a few short weeks away. This journey took me approximately 2500 miles away from home—Seattle to Atlanta (specifically Loganville, GA, which is a place I had never even heard of, I might add). I had never even met these people in person. Prior to going, I did not know anyone who would be in attendance at the conference. I was asked countless times how I could just go places like that, by myself. My response is always, "I know no strangers in God's Kingdom." I knew I would be among my siblings in Christ. And on another note, when you are chasing after your destiny and chasing after God, sometimes you just need to travel a little light.

I began to sense it would not just be running to another conference. I had done that for years on end. Had a great experience each time, but the hype always faded rather quickly upon my return home. This time, however, I sensed whatever was to take place at this NBRN event would prove to be a life-changing, spiritual-awakening moment for me. Each time I came across the theme of the conference, *Pressing Into the Prophetic Shift,* it shook me to my core.

Allow me to attempt to recap my encounter:

Day #1…Though I had been up since 3 AM, had flown all day from the West to the East Coast; had spent hours in traffic to get to the venue; I dug in with reckless abandon. I have come to a place where I realize it is NOT about me and ALL about HIM! In that very place…God met me. I left Elijah's Altar (the conference venue) that night completely drunk in the Holy Ghost.

Day #2…Prior to arriving at the conference, God had already confirmed I needed to fully align with this ministry. So without hesitation, I made the commitment. I was commissioned as a Radical Revivalist and welcomed into the New Breed Revival Network family, was prayed over, and received a strong prophetic word from the Lord. That night, in the final session for the evening, I said goodbye to Yolanda (as I knew her) as she died…right there on Elijah's Altar. I rose up as a brand new person, ready to step into the fullness of who God called me to be.

Day #3…I returned for what most would consider a conclusion of the whole matter. But I chose to deem it to be a continuation. I had come alive and left the conference ready to dig deeper…to run farther and faster…to steward the fire that had begun to burn within me again.

> *To every thing there is a season, and a time to every purpose under the heaven…"*
>
> **Ecclesiastes 3:1 (KJV)**

For years, I sought the Lord, pleading with Him, about bringing those into my world who could not only help me to understand the calling on my life. I knew I also needed to be connected to those who would be an example of how to execute and be willing to help me walk it out. I now realize God's timing is perfect. Truth be told, years ago, I did not just want those who would run alongside me…I wanted those who would run for me. Thankfully, God had my number and knew what was best for me. And I am so grateful I now know I have what it takes to run my own race…and God can now trust me with the relay team He has always had in store for me!

That one act of obedience to *GO* not only led me to a family of people who would run the race with me, but also to a long awaited answer to prayer. For years, I prayed and sought God about who my spiritual parents are, those He would have me fully submit to as my spiritual authority. When God told me to get to this event, I had no idea I would meet my spiritual father, Apostle Ryan LeStrange, at that meeting. Shortly after the conference, I aligned with TRIBE Network, the ministry he founded as a home for those called to one of the five-fold ministry offices. I met his lovely wife, Apostle Joy, later in the year…and yes that relationship fit like a glove too. Over the last year I have lived in awe of how He has allowed this to unfold, be confirmed and is continuing to stamp His seal of approval on what He has ordained. I now even lead the RLM Prayer Shield, Apostle Ryan's team of intercessors; which covers him, his family and all aspects of his ministries in prayer. Through this experience, I learned a very important truth. A simple response to *GO* could be an absolute key to unlocking destiny in every area of our lives, including relationships.

BLESSING #2
TURNING THE TABLES

The LORD will open the heavens, the storehouse of his bounty, to send rain on your land in season and to bless all the work of your hands. You will lend to many nations but will borrow from none. The LORD will make you the head, not the tail. If you pay attention to the commands of the LORD your God that I give you this day and carefully follow them, you will always be at the top, never at the bottom.

Deuteronomy 28:12-13 (NIV)

Regardless of where life has taken you over the years, God has a plan for you to live in total freedom and prosperity. Many have experienced poverty in childhood and even into adulthood. Many have lived under the shadows of the past and the curses of their natural bloodline. Many have just accepted their circumstances simply because they are familiar with it and assume that is their portion. But allow me to serve notice on the enemy of your mind. It is not God's will for you to experience lack in any area of your life. Despite your upbringing, your status shifted when you joined the family of God. Therefore, it is time that you begin to live out on earth what God has already declared in heaven.

Your kingdom come, your will be done, on earth as it is in heaven.

Matthew 6:10 (NIV)

In heaven you are blessed beyond measure, as the focal verse of Scripture points out. Yes the Lord is prepared to open the heavens to you. It is a matter of rightly positioning yourself as one who truly belongs to Him, and endeavoring to walk upright before Him. In essence, it is not a matter of where you come from but rather a matter of where you are in the Kingdom currently...and where you will *GO* as God sends you. Your willingness to heed His voice and follow His commands will not only unlock many doors unto you, but will also turn the tables such that you will step out of the land of not enough and into the realm of more than enough. And not only will it be evident to you, but also to those all around you.

> *But you are a chosen people, a royal priesthood, a holy nation, a people for God's own possession, to proclaim the virtues of Him who called you out of darkness into His marvelous light.*
>
> **1 Peter 2:9 (BSB)**

Here is my transparent tables-turning story. I did not come from a background of having much. My parents and their parents did not either. While my father did all he could to give us the best of everything, I had no idea what the cost was beyond what I could see. Most of the time, as a child, we had a really nice vehicle. Also, my father was very skillful in the area of construction. So even though when I was born, I went home to a tiny two bedroom trailer; it evolved into a beautiful home over the years. My mother decorated with the best of everything. When we entered teen years, appearance was everything to my older sister and me. As such, when we went school shopping each year, we knew what we wanted; and my father was determined to oblige every one of our heart's desires. What I did not know, at the time, is we really could not afford half of what we took home from the stores. Most of what we got was financed through credit of some sort.

As I got older, I began to realize we were struggling just like the next family. Although my parents did the best they could, they had no concept of making wise financial decisions. Living in debt was a way of life for most, including them—us. Eventually I began to realize we were not as well off as I had thought. At one time we had a vehicle repossessed, which completely confused me since we seemed to have it all together. While I did not question my parents, I knew something was not right about how we were living. As a matter of fact, I had to learn the value of financial integrity on my own. Though I was not yet a Christian when I left home, God was clearly grooming me to become who He designed me to be. Even before making the decision to serve Him, I was learning to have a Kingdom mindset.

When I surrendered my life to Christ, I quickly learned the blessing of walking in the will of God. As a result, my world quickly began to shift. Yes, the tables began to turn for me. It was not that I was completely debt free at that moment or anything, but it was evident I was not living beneath the same dark cloud of bad financial decisions I had grown up under. I remember planning out how I would become debt free. Also, I could remember getting so close to that goal only to find myself right back in the debt trap. There was a time I paid off all of my credit card debts, old medical bills, etc. This might be considered a reason to celebrate, except the sole purpose was to get back into debt purchasing the vehicle of my choice, which was far more than I could afford to spend at that time. I remember the day I sat across the table from the car salesman. He looked at my credit report that I had worked an entire year to clean up. He said, "Wow, are you trying to buy a house or something?" I crossed my legs and said, "Nope, I'll just take my Toyota 4Runner for now!" I had spent a year in Korea. While everyone shopped to their heart's content, I sent home pre-addressed payments to my bill collectors. All that wisdom thrown out the window with one decision to take on even more debt with the purchase of one item.

I was destined to be free from debt is true. However, it would take action on my part to realize that freedom. It was not until I learned of giving to the Kingdom of God and the blessings that follow when doing so. As a baby Christian only weeks into accepting Jesus as Lord of my life, I was introduced to giving like I had never seen before. I had gotten caught up in a thirty day revival. A variety of speakers passed through…prophets, evangelists, pastors.

Each night people gave liberally. Me, being new to this type of atmosphere, I knew no better. Ironically, that is the best thing that could have happened to me. I did not question who was false or real, good or bad. I just gave out of obedience. I gave as unto the Lord. And He honored that. I discovered three things giving out of obedience does:

1. Unlocks financial blessings.
2. Unlocks wisdom with finances.
3. Turns the tables concerning your financial status.

Abraham, whom God eventually promoted and renamed from Abram, knew the blessing of giving according to God's expectation, even without full understanding of the circumstances. As you will read in Scripture, there was not even real clarity about who this Melchizedek person was. Yet Abraham knew God, and deferred to His expectations rather than his own limited thinking. Abraham knew by way of God's promises, that he was already destined for greater; but he was careful to honor the Lord's requirements to unlock a continuous flow of blessings that was in store for him. Let us take a look at how Abraham entreated Melchizedek, the priest.

Melchizedek was king of Salem and priest of the Highest God. He met Abraham, who was returning from "the royal massacre," and gave him his blessing. Abraham in turn gave him a tenth of the spoils. "Melchizedek" means "King of Righteousness." "Salem" means "Peace." So, he is also "King of Peace." Melchizedek towers out of the past—without record of family ties, no account of beginning or end. In this way he is like the Son of God, one huge priestly presence dominating the landscape always.

You realize just how great Melchizedek is when you see that Father Abraham gave him a tenth of the captured treasure. Priests descended from Levi are commanded by law to collect tithes from the people, even though they are all more or less equals, priests and people, having a common father in Abraham. But this man, a complete outsider, collected tithes from Abraham and blessed him, the one to whom the promises had been given. In acts of blessing, the lesser is blessed by the greater.

Hebrews 7:1-7 (MSG)

Here we see Melchizedek just appears on the scene, with no proof of where he came from or who he really is, even referred to as "a complete outsider". He is validated by Abraham's willingness to give to him as unto God. Many struggle with the notion of giving, especially tithing. There is this misconception that we are giving our hard earned money to a man or woman. Bringing the tithes to the House of God (See Malachi 3:10), as we are commanded to do so is more about us than about those who are collecting it. It is about the act of obedience that has the potential to unlock manifold blessings.

It actually saddens me to see many who live beneath their means because they lack understanding of this very principle. When you hold back your tithes, you are not withholding something from man. You are obstructing what God wants to release to you. You cannot imagine the measure of blessings that are in store for you when you release what rightfully belongs to God as a simple act of obedience. For many, there is fear there will not be enough finances to do what you need (want) to do if you give God what He requires. NEWS FLASH: Giving God what is rightfully His will not dam up your finances, your disobedience is what does that. Whoops…I am thinking I should have written this topic in a later chapter. But I hope you will stay with me here. Here is my account of how giving according to God's word turned the tables for me.

As I indicated, I learned to give during a revival. I chuckle at the thought of not knowing what any of those revivalists are doing today. I did, however, keep in touch with a family who was attending the church where I received a prophetic word that shook me to the core. It was that word that sent me home knowing I had to surrender my life to Christ. When I contacted my friends one year later, just checking in, I learned the pastor of that church (who happens to be the one to give me a word of knowledge that led to me surrendering my life to Christ) experienced a moral failure and had fallen away from the church for a season. Was I devastated hearing that? Yes. Did I fall away from God because of it? No. Did I stop giving because this "man" had fallen from grace? No. Did God continue to bless me for every act of obedience in giving? Yes…He did and continues to bless me beyond measure to this very day!

Just in case you think I always had money to give, I assure you that was not the case…far from it! My former husband was an addict. We were separated twice; and eventually divorced. That scenario left me with grown up bills and no support of any kind. When I found myself in situations like not knowing how I would pay my mortgage, utilities, credit card bills, buy food and whatever else my children needed; I still treated tithing as a nonnegotiable. No way was I going to follow every other instruction God gave me and miss the fullness of His promises by not obeying in this one little area of my life.

My situation was this, and probably yours too: If I give it, there won't be enough, but I can rest easy in obedience. If I don't give it, I will still come up short and be found standing outside of God's will. Sadly many today still choose the latter. Not me. I chose to give by faith. As a result, I have NEVER gone without anything I need and God sees fit to give me a whole lot of what I want too. To date, I have never had to pay a mortgage late. There was always enough for me to pay my bills on time. Confession: Sometimes I was late because I forgot; which is not God's fault, right? But that is another story. I paid off my vehicle. My children and I were able to take amazing vacations, and not have to finance them to remain on credit cards. As a matter of fact, God increased my wisdom with debt management. While it is recommended to not have credit cards open, I do. However, most have set on a zero balance for years. The debt, with the exception of my home, I did incur was due to poor decisions of the past, and is finally going to all be paid off in a few short months.

Who knew obeying a simple principle on giving could turn the tables in this way? If you struggle with the principle of giving, particularly tithing, you should really lean into God for greater understanding. May He flood you with revelation concerning this topic. May you come into the knowledge of what is available to you when you become enlightened by the truth. Finally, may the tables-turning anointing and season be upon you now…In Jesus' Name.

Yolanda Perry

BLESSING #3
ALL IN THE FAMILY

They replied, "Believe in the Lord Jesus and you will be saved, along with everyone in your household."

Acts 16:31 (NLT)

When we enter into the Kingdom of God, we position ourselves to receive an inheritance from our Heavenly Father. Inheritance can be defined as that which passes on from one individual to another upon death—property, titles, debts, rights, and obligations. Since the King owes no one, we do not have to worry about the debts and obligations part, only that which will edify and add value to our lives. Specifically, I would like to talk about our "rights" to expect our children and our children's children to receive salvation, just as we have. While I will focus on children, please note this could apply to anyone we hold dear, as our inheritance can be passed to anyone we choose. So, apply the message in this segment to anyone you determine to also reap the blessings for which you have sown prayers for. It is simply common for parents to pass theirs on to their offspring, but not exclusive by any means.

Though our inheritance rightly belongs to our children, they are not always in proper alignment to receive it. As such, we just have to believe God will preserve our blessings for them as we await their return to Him. Oftentimes people get weary, waiting for the promises of God to manifest concerning their loved ones. At other times, parents sometimes unwisely bestow blessings upon their children prematurely; and the children prove through their behavior they are not ready for what they have received. In either case, God never goes back on His word. His promises are yes and amen (See 2 Corinthians 1:20). Even in their dysfunction, God's plan is still sure for their lives. Though it tarries, wait for it, for it shall surely come (See Habakkuk 2:3).

Imagine how the father of the prodigal son felt when his baby boy took off after having received his portion of his earthly inheritance. He went off to enjoy life and squandered it all. What he did not know was the Father's love was part of the fullness of his inheritance as well. He just wanted to party and live in the moment. He was blinded by what seemed like the good life at the time, as many sons and daughters are. But let's look at how this father responded to the matter.

> *And he said, "There was a man who had two sons. And the younger of them said to his father, 'Father, give me the share of property that is coming to me.' And he divided his property between them. Not many days later, the younger son gathered all he had and took a journey into a far country, and there he squandered his property in reckless living. And when he had spent everything, a severe famine arose in*

that country, and he began to be in need...And he arose and came to his father. But while he was still a long way off, his father saw him and felt compassion, and ran and embraced him and kissed him. And the son said to him, 'Father, I have sinned against heaven and before you. I am no longer worthy to be called your son. But the father said... "let us eat and celebrate. For this my son was dead, and is alive again; he was lost, and is found." And they began to celebrate.

Luke 15:11-14; 20-24 (ESV)

If the prodigal's father was anything like me, he was probably thinking he could kick himself for giving all those valuables and monies to his son prematurely. He probably beat himself up at first, weighing out how different the outcome might have been if he had held back what he released. He likely wondered where he went wrong in how he raised this kid, and what would make him turn away from his family and from God. Judging by the outcome,

I sensed that, at some point, this father got it. At some point, he allowed God to minister to his heart concerning his offspring. At some point, he just believed God would bring his son home; and he let God prepare his heart for whenever his son would return. I imagine God instructing this dad in his darkest hour…and the words are something like, "Don't fret. Don't worry. Don't give up. Keep believing. Keep standing on My promises for your offspring. Keep *GO*-ing!" And he did. And as we read in the finale…his son returned and they got to celebrate. And so shall this be your story too.

Here is mine.

My children's upbringing was challenging for sure. Much of their lives they witnessed such dysfunction in our household as I endeavored to walk out the will of God concerning my marriage. They lived through two very traumatic separations, then divorce and all that happened in between; which I will not lay out in detail here. As you can imagine, however, this caused them to question the realness and love of God, who would allow us to bear all we did. While I endured the pain of a broken marriage, I could never ignore the fact that they were living through the pain of our family unraveling. Though I had witnessed many families falling apart and their children going astray because of it, I was determined that would not be the end story for my offspring. God had given me a glimpse of His plan for each of their lives, and without knowing how it could or would come to fruition; I stayed in God's face, begging Him to show me my part in it all. His instruction to me was: "You keep *GO*-ing and show them what it looks like to be faithful to me. I will do the rest." Those are not the exact words, but that was my takeaway from my conversation with God concerning the future of my offspring in the Kingdom.

God also made a very specific promise to me that my children would not only be saved, but they would also walk alongside me in ministry. Let me be honest and tell you my children did not just decide to serve Jesus. At the time He spoke those words to me, that was far out. Nothing about what I was seeing from my children gave me reason to believe what God had said to me would come to pass. They were in their teen years, living it out as though they were professionals who wrote the manual for it. With the exception of one of my children, who was pursuing a relationship with God as best she knew how, signs from the other two—their behavior and mindsets—left me with little to no hope at all.

Surely, I made many mistakes in parenting; trying to lord over them, tell them what to do, condemning them for their mistakes, all in failed attempts to convince them to get with my idea of God's plan for them. Nothing I tried to do to help along God's plan succeeded. To be honest, I made the process much more difficult than it had to be. I was already doing what needed to be done, by simply living for God as best I knew how. My children did not need a lecture, they needed an example. Who knew just continuing to press on in my pursuit with Jesus would be the thing to eventually allow their hearts to turn toward Him as well.

It would not be truthful for me to say stepping up as the spiritual head of my household was easy. Having a man-child made it that much more difficult, as I questioned my inadequacy and whether I could pour into him what he needed. Again, I had to defer to God for divine instructions on how to walk this out. As usual, in His still small voice, He pointed me back to what He had already said.

> ...*then trust the Lord completely; don't ever trust yourself. In everything you do, put God first, and he will direct you and crown your efforts with success.*
>
> **Proverbs 3:5-6 (TLB)**

Now that verse right there is shout-worthy! But I must keep writing to meet my deadline. Even while living through one of the most difficult circumstances, I centered my attention on God's requirement of me, to show my children what it looks like to live for Him. For many years it seemed it made no difference; it seemed my efforts were in vain. Yet I continued to press on. I continued to pray. I continued to remind God of what He promised along the way as well. Though I believed, my prayers even began to seem hopeless to me. And looking at some of the actions of my kids, it appeared it would not happen. But God kept reminding me to keep *GO*-ing. I kept hearing the echoing remnants of a particular verse, "Though it tarries, wait for it, for it shall surely come." (See Habakkuk 2:3)

After years of standing in faith, my son walked away from God. One daughter believed in God, but her lifestyle would not have suggested it to say the least. I found myself in major spiritual warfare over their souls. If I judged by what I saw in the natural, I would faint and declare it was not worth it. However, the glimpse of what would be was enough to convince me to walk in obedience to God and trust Him with the finished product. So I did.

Suddenly, God began to turn things around. This year I shared my birthday with my son, who is no longer a prodigal, but is now living for Jesus, and is in hot pursuit of walking in obedience as well! I will never forget the night he called. I was in bed winding down from a long day and pondering how special that day felt, even though nothing really special had happened at that point. My son had brought me gifts to my job earlier in the day, with birthday wishes; so, I did not anticipate a phone call. The short of the story is that by the end of the conversation he wanted me to lead him back to Christ.

BEST BIRTHDAY EVER!!!

I had just come into relationship with a church after having been invited to a conference there. I thought it would be the perfect place for my son to attend. He joined. Later in the year, my middle child visited a young adult's group with her brother. She transitioned to that church as well. Around the same time God reminded me of a prophetic word He had given me at the conference I attended. Several months earlier, while at that conference, I had written it in my journal. Basically, God had told me that church was my home as well. He said I did not have to do anything, but He would make it happen. As such, I transitioned to the church with my kids; and we are now all worshiping in the same House. Not only that, as God has been birthing out my ministry over the last year; and just as you read earlier, God's promise that my children will be walking right alongside me every step of the way is surely being fulfilled. They are excited about what God is doing in my life and how they get to be part of this move of God taking place.

In my times of brokenness and despair, I kept *GO*-ing after God without fail. Radical obedience became my pursuit, even in times of helplessness and hopelessness. I kept hearkening to His still small voice. He kept His word to me. He came through for my family. And I know full well He will do the same for yours too! Lean in for his *GO* instruction to you and do it, whatever IT may be. The result can only be that He will be faithful to respond to you in just the same way He did to me. Remember, it is not just about you. Your family needs you to obey God. Others do too.

BLESSING #4
POSITIONED FOR PROMOTION

The authority to reward someone does not come from the east, from the west, or even from the wilderness. God alone is the judge. He punishes one person and rewards another.

Psalm 75:6-7 (GW)

It is a natural thing to pursue promotions on a job, whether it is in the corporate world, labor industry, ministry, or any other line of work. We should all seek progression in every area of our lives, including employment. However, we should also look forward to and even expect promotion in the realm of the Spirit when we are walking in obedience to God. When we listen to His still small voice, elevation and upgrade are inevitable. The exciting thing is when God grants promotions in the Spirit, He has a habit of making a big deal about it in the natural realm too. He loves to showcase when He blesses and pours favor upon the lives of His children. He does not hold back.

For the LORD God is a sun and shield; the LORD bestows favor and honor. No good thing does he withhold from those who walk uprightly.

Psalm 84:11 (ESV)

I might be the only mom who will admit my son is not perfect, never has been and never will be. However, I will confess I thought he was when I gave birth to him. You should have seen that cute little face, those cute little fingers and toes. You get the drift. Well, it only took a few unexplained screams and screeches in the middle of the night, accompanied by a few untimely diaper-demands for me to realize he definitely has flaws. Years into it, when certain other challenges arose, the earlier inconveniences did not seem so bad after all. Nevertheless, I loved him unconditionally, just like God does.

My son, Darius, was in second grade when I committed my life to the Lord. As most new Christians I was full of zeal and over-the-top in love with Jesus. I could not get enough of Christian television. It was constantly playing throughout my house. I remember it like it was yesterday. During this time, Darius was mostly intrigued by televangelist Rod Parsley's ministry. He loved when he laid hands on people and they were slain in the Spirit. If you let me tell it, I would say he probably did not even miss his cartoons at all. Never mind there was no option when I had Christian programing on. And no need asking his recollection of this season in our home life.

Regardless, during this time Darius came to know God in a deeply personal way. He not only made the decision to commit his life to Christ, but also was baptized in the Holy Spirit with the evidence of speaking in other tongues. He experienced this right in my living room.

And you guessed it...this happened right by my very own Spirit-filled TV. I wish I could say my son was perfect in every way from this day forward. Quite the contrary. This broke open a season of initiation to warfare, something I would come to learn much about. My son instantly became a threat and target to hell all at the same time. He began to experience his own unbelievable spiritual attacks that continued through adolescence and even into his adult life.

As with all of my children, Darius was in church as long as he lived at home with me. Eventually he was out on his own. Not knowing or having the strength to fight against the ongoing spiritual attacks, Darius found himself completely detached from the ways and will of God, living as a prodigal. During this time, I still loved my son and supported him according to God's leading. It was the most difficult thing to witness his life deteriorate so rapidly and not be able to do anything about it, except pray and trust God's plan and promise for him.

It has been a year and a half since I led my son, my firstborn, back to the Lord (See *Blessing #3, All In The Family*). As I stated earlier, I considered my birthday to be a really good day. But at the time, I had no idea how much better it was about to get. That night when Darius called, I knew within seconds of hearing his voice that something unsettling was happening in his world. As we talked through what was going on, at the time, I just began to speak words of life and love to his spirit. He knew what he needed and was wide open to step right back into the life Christ died for him to have. The short of this story is this mom slept really good that night; and as declared in *Blessing #3*, it is worth saying again…that was my best birthday ever!

From the time Darius recommitted his life, he endeavored to serve God wholeheartedly. It was clear to see he wanted to be all-in concerning his walk with the Lord. Right away he got plugged into a local church and started trying to build relationships with other believers. This was a challenge since he had struggled for so many years trying to navigate unhealthy relationships. It was a foreign concept to engage in healthy ones. Nonetheless, he has stayed the course. And God has honored his pursuit of Him, and has proven his immeasurable amount of grace and mercy for Darius, as with all of His children who endeavor to walk upright before Him.

But he said to me, "My grace is sufficient for you, for my power is made perfect in weakness."

2 Corinthian 12:9a (NIV)

The faithful love of the LORD never ends! His mercies never cease. Great is his faithfulness; his mercies begin afresh each morning.

Lamentations 3:22-23 (NIV)

Second Corinthians 12:9 is such an encouraging reminder that it is not God's expectation that we be perfect in all our ways. When we fall short, His grace takes up the slack; and His power is perfected within us.

Then there's more. The next morning God pretends as though yesterday's shortcomings did not even happen so to speak. He releases brand new mercies, along with a fresh start, another chance to begin again.

Who would not serve a God like that?

Since Darius's time of recommitment, I witnessed Darius strive to live and walk upright. I also have had a front row seat at the productions where many of his performances were less than stellar-worthy. Yet the remarkable thing was seeing him continue running to the House of God, seeking forgiveness and guidance. I watched his frustration, which I translated as conviction, over making the same mistakes as he did in the past. Yet he did not drown in that place of sorrow. Over and over, again and again, he ran back to the House. Each time, I saw evident growth in him. At the same time, my heart smiled as he began to recognize the increase of favor upon his own life. The kind of favor that brings promotion. I will conclude *Blessing #4,*

Positioned for Promotion with Darius's most recent testimony of promotion.

Darius was employed at Lakewood Ford years ago as a salesman. He did not really fit in that field, but rather than releasing him, he was offered a different position in the company. Eventually he was laid off. For over two years Darius tried to find suitable employment. This was during the time he was living life as a prodigal. Shortly after he maxed out his unemployment benefits, Lakewood Ford offered him his job back. In a short period of time, Darius received small promotions, and even what he considered to be his dream schedule. He started having some trouble with unfair treatment and working in a bit of a hostile environment. Despite this, Darius kept his head up and did what he had to do, understanding he has to do whatever he must to take care of himself, and provide support for his children.

Tension continued to build, even while Darius was away on vacation. When he returned, the company had hired someone new in his department. As lead, Darius trained the gentleman. To his surprise, he soon discovered he was training his replacement. At the end of the week, Darius was fired with no reasonable explanation. I remember getting the call, thinking…and even said aloud a few times, "You have got to be kidding me." Well, he was not. Quickly I shifted my train of thought and told him not to worry, because God has this too and NOTHING would go lacking.

A series of misfortunes had happened in his world over the past couple of months, and even specifically that day. His car was vandalized. And even without proof, he was certain who had done it. This blow compounded his frustration. But I knew God would come through for him greatly. This was a Friday. The Sunday that followed, Darius was given an indirect prophetic word about someone getting an open door with a promotion in 10 days. Our pastor, James Ludlow, had given that word earlier, in a setting where Darius was not present. And his wife, Tammy, mentioned it to Darius when she heard what happened with his job. I remember her saying something like she sensed this was a word for Darius.

Darius embraced what she said. However, it was a struggle for him the days that followed, not sure what he would do. I continued to encourage him and talk through strategies for him to make it financially while in transition with his job misfortune. During that time, we had many talks, but one such conversation I treasure greatly. Darius shared how he was talking to God about his situation, and then clearly heard God's voice speak back to him. Here is what he heard:

"If you sacrifice something for me, I will not only bless you, but it will be with increase."

Pardon me while I take a praise break! Now pardon me while I relocate because Starbucks thinks I am too disruptive! Just kidding…but close call.

When God made this proposal to Darius, he knew exactly what God wanted him to sacrifice. Without hesitation, he did agree to partner with God concerning this instruction. I am being vague, preserving the opportunity for him to write the specifics in his own book. Yes. I just prophesied that over my son's destiny. According to Darius, he had many temptations that threatened his allegiance to this commitment he had made. But he stood firm. It was a little over a week, and Darius had no solid prospects for a job. He was still a bit discouraged, but standing strong in spite of it all. A former coworker reached out to him and told him of an open position. Darius went and pursued it, only to be turned down. He was positive though, understanding that what God has for him is for him.

The following day, after being turned down, Darius was called back by the same company and hired on the spot. But wait, there's more:

- His new schedule is even better than the one he had at Lakewood Ford.

- He not only received an increase in pay, it was even more than what he could

get Lakewood Ford to agree to pay him as a lead in his department.
- This all happened on the 10th day, in line with the prophetic word given by Pastor James Ludlow.

- Because of a windfall of a blessing Darius received just weeks earlier, he even had enough to sustain him such that it would be as though he never missed a day of work in between.

No doubt the lapse in employment and uncertainty was a bit much for Darius to bear. Yet he stood in faith, endeavoring to honor and serve God as best he could. That is exactly the mindset that qualified him for favor, set him up for increase, and positioned him for promotion. That is what we can all expect when we follow this model…and His still small voice!

BLESSING #5

FINANCIAL FLOODGATES OPEN

"Give, and it will be given to you. They will pour into your lap a good measure -- pressed down, shaken together, and running over. For by your standard of measure it will be measured to you in return."

Luke 6:38 (NASB)

For some, the most challenging spiritual discipline to walk in is that of giving according to God's Word. There is even still much controversy around whether tithing is relevant today. I am not one to be defensive about or debate whether God's Word is true. I can only testify of my own accounts of what takes place as a result of my obedience to give sacrificially, to sow unsparingly, and yes…to tithe as an act of obedience. For as long as I have been serving God (this December will mark 20 years of salvation for me), I have experienced His unprecedented favor over my finances. No doubt it is because I learned the principles of giving early on, and followed them to the letter. As such, I am reaping the benefits thereof. Yet I understand many were not privy to the lessons I learned and still find it to be a great struggle to grasp the concept of sowing and reaping, just like the rich young ruler who put more value on his possessions than eternal life.

> *As he went out into the street, a man came running up, greeted him with great reverence, and asked, "Good Teacher, what must I do to get eternal life?" Jesus said, "Why are you calling me good? No one is good, only God. You know the commandments: Don't murder, don't commit adultery, don't steal, don't lie, don't cheat, honor your father and mother." He said, "Teacher,*

I have—from my youth—kept them all!" Jesus looked him hard in the eye—and loved him! He said, "There's one thing left: Go sell whatever you own and give it to the poor. All your wealth will then be heavenly wealth. And come follow me." The man's face clouded over. This was the last thing he expected to hear, and he walked off with a heavy heart. He was holding on tight to a lot of things, and not about to let go.

Mark 10:17-22 (MSG)

How sad is that for a person to be so attached to worldly possessions that will serve him no purpose in heaven. Good grief, I would even give up my elephant collection to get into heaven. You would have to know how much I love elephants to know how huge of a sacrifice that would be for me. Well, enough of my dry humor. Let us seriously explore this rich young ruler's quandary for a moment. He is not alone in this. Have you ever been prompted by the Holy Spirit to give outside of your comfort level? I have. Did you delay it, ignore it, or do it? For me, I have done all of the above at one time or another. And I can tell you in no uncertain terms that doing exactly what God prompts me to do always results in blessings beyond measure for my family and me.

While this scripture is speaking of giving for eternal purposes, there are people who have just as difficult a time releasing financial seeds now in anticipation of an earthly harvest. Many have even seen what God has done in the lives of others through giving, yet still are skeptical and unwilling to take God at His word. If you are one who is not yet convinced giving opens you up to blessings, I hope my story will not only enlighten you, but also provoke you to take God's challenge in Malachi 3:10. Obedience in giving, especially of the tithe, is sure to open financial floodgates for you.

> *Bring all the tithes into the storehouse so there will be enough food in my Temple. If you do," says the LORD of Heaven's Armies, "I will open the windows of heaven for you. I will pour out a blessing so great you won't have*

enough room to take it in! Try it! Put me to the test!

Malachi 3:10 (NLT)

Part of my story involves my former husband relapsing into the life of drug addiction more than once. As a result, I endured two separations before my marriage landed on the steps of the courthouse, ending in divorce. If you know of anyone who has been negatively impacted by the effects of a drug addicted loved one, you have a bit of a glimpse into my world with no need for me to exaggerate the circumstances. Not to mention, when my former husband left, I had three children glaring at me as if to say, "Now what are we going to do?!"

My action plan was simple—to just obey God no matter what. And that is exactly what I did, especially in terms of giving. When marital separation became my reality, it happened at the most inopportune time—as if there is ever a good time for your mate to check out on you.

To put into context what I mean, here was my reality in living color:

1. I was a fulltime college student.

2. I was a disabled veteran, and only had a work study position.

3. We had recently purchased our home, now having a mortgage payment.

4. We had charged furniture on a credit card, with intent to pay off in six months.

5. I would now have to figure out how to pay all household utilities and take care of all the kids' needs on my own.

6. Finally, there is no such thing as receiving spousal support or child support when drug addiction is in the equation.

Though the synopsis above was my reality, I still trusted God's promises concerning giving. One Sunday, as I sat in church, as the offering was collected. I was broken and completely embarrassed about the fact that my husband was no longer sitting next to me. I started to engage in a conversation with God in my heart. Though I knew I could possibly lose everything, not knowing how my bills would be paid, I was determined to not allow tithe to be an optional thing. From my small disability check and earnings from work study, I would give the tenth no matter what.

Then I was a little grieved over the notion that I could not give a general offering beyond that, because there was a certain amount we, as a family, had been giving weekly without fail. So, as I sat there having my little heart to heart with God, I said to Him, "If you give it to me…I promise I will give it back to You." I was so serious about this vow, that I took out my pocket calendar and started a little ritual. Every Sunday during offering time, I pulled it out and marked off the amount I owed God for that vow. Weeks and months went by as the amount was increasing with no breakthrough in sight.

One day I was talking to my older sister. We were fantasizing about me coming home, bringing the kids and having this elaborate 8-week summer vacation. Because of my accounting background, I made a budget just for fun. Including the coverage of my bills for the summer, travel to my city of origin, and the excursions we were considering, I estimated I needed at least ten thousand dollars. Good grief, it might as well had been ten million. Either way it seemed insurmountable to attain. I told my sister the amount in another of our fun conversations. We laughed as we dreamed together across the miles.

I shall never forget the day I went to the mailbox and pulled out a huge yellow envelope. Again, I was on the phone with my sister and started joking that it must be a government check, even though the envelope's size did not fit the profile. Nonetheless, my laughter turned into screams as I read the letter inside. My veteran's disability had increased. Though it was not by a substantial amount at the time, the Veteran's Administration had decided to give me back pay for two years, from the time I had initially submitted my claim. Yes…the floodgates had opened. In three days, the sum total of $10,854 was in my bank account just like that. Glory!

No doubt God honored not only my obedience, but also my willingness to sacrifice. And just in case you are wondering, I did keep my word. Tithing on that windfall of a blessing was automatic. But remember that vow I made each Sunday I pulled out my pocket calendar. Well, it was over $700 when that breakthrough came. And I gave every penny of it…cheerfully!

> *You must each decide in your heart how much to give. And don't give reluctantly or in response to pressure. "For God loves a person who gives cheerfully." And God will generously provide all you need. Then you will always have everything you need and plenty left over to share with others.*
>
> **2 Corinthians 9:7-8 (NLT)**

Giving, for me, was a saving grace so to speak. God never suffered me to want for anything, not even a vacation. For some that might seem trivial or wasteful, but my children relied on that for a sense of normalcy in the midst of our shattered world. Not only that, it taught each of them the faithfulness of God through the discipline of giving. To this day my children each know the benefits of giving all too well. I still have the duplicate of the first tithe check my youngest daughter wrote when she was just eight years old. She is now eighteen in her second year of pre-med, studying to become a pediatrician…and she is still a tither today. Many of her friends had to call it quits in their first year due to finances. Yet God is supernaturally providing one scholarship and grant at a time for her education. Not only that, I am still in my home…and the deed says, "Yolanda C. Perry". I have never had to miss a mortgage payment. My vehicle was paid off years ago. No utilities or credit card bill had to go lacking. And best of all, my children and I have not had to forgo any vacations!

While I am not rich, and have some rather tall goals to reach financially; I will say God has truly let the financial floodgates open and flow freely for me. Did you know the same gesture is available to you? If you are not living in bountiful blessings, that God kind of abundance; I am simply trying to encourage you to believe you can. As you have read one account of what God did through my giving (more in other highlighted blessings), I challenge you to expect God to do the same for you, through your obedience. Yes...imagine how you, too, can experience the hand of God moving upon you, your finances, kicking open floodgates in your life too!

Now *GO* beyond your imagination. GIVE according to His word...and expect it.

BLESSING #6
CALL-IN CONVERSION CLAIMS

Who do you think Paul is, anyway? Or Apollos, for that matter? Servants, both of us—servants who waited on you as you gradually learned to entrust your lives to our mutual Master. We each carried out our servant assignment. I planted the seed, Apollos watered the plants, but God made you grow. It's not the one who plants or the one who waters who is at the center of this process but God, who makes things grow. Planting and watering are menial servant jobs at minimum wages. What makes them worth doing is the God we are serving. You happen to be God's field in which we are working.

1 Corinthians 3:5-9 (MSG)

As with giving, evangelism is another discipline that has been unpopular, misunderstood and even neglected in many ways. We live amongst a culture that needs instant gratification, craving to see the fruit of our labor NOW. However, evangelism offers no guaranteed outcome...or does it? In some cases, you can witness for hours, sharing the love of Jesus, and find yourself feeling completely defeated when your offer of salvation is declined. It is even more so disappointing when you saw a certain facial expression or body language that suggested your potential new convert has been won over, as though it is a done deal, then nothing. Or so you think nothing happened. The fact that someone does not make the decision to follow Christ immediately after you have ministered to them is not an indicator that your ministry is not effective. It is simply a reminder that you are not the Savior; you are only the messenger—seed planter, or perhaps a seed waterer as Paul and Apollos were.

I love how the Message Bible lays out the above verses in 1 Corinthians Chapter 3. It is made clear that Paul and Apollos were mere ministers and should not be esteemed any higher than that. Their primary job was to respond in obedience to God, complete whatever ministry assignments were placed before them, and leave the deal closings up to God. While Paul and Apollos were very instrumental in the process of leading people to follow Christ, they were clear on the roles they played, planting and watering. They in no way sought recognition for what they did; they gave all the glory to God. They were selfless in their ambition of doing God's work, and were blessed by the witness of what God accomplished through their obedience to Him. When God said *GO*, they went, they planted and watered; and the conversions through God's handiwork was worth every act of obedience to Him. Their primary pursuit was that of honoring God and the saving of souls; for all to come to know Christ...and calling in new converts...those conversion claims! Yes. They knew God should get all the glory. But they were co-laborers with God, an integral part of leading people to Him. The fruit of their evangelism efforts brought them great joy as well when God brought in the increase.

In my first book, *Worth the Wait*, I tell my story of how a young woman went door to door on the military base where I lived, evangelizing. She was a neighbor to me. In relation to the scriptures above, I consider her to be a modern day Paul, a planter. She was obedient to God's *GO*! She was clear about her assignment to the Body of Christ, never growing weary; and never wavering. To this day I marvel at her tenacity. Clearly it was all about God and not about herself. If it were the other way around, she would have been so discouraged by the rejection she faced, that she would not do what she did day after day, week after week. Who is this committed one? Tammie is her name.

Tammie went to people's houses, knocked on the door, and asked for an opportunity to tell them about Jesus. This is a norm for Jehovah's Witnesses and Mormons, but not so much for

Christians. At least it was an unfamiliar concept to me. Having grown up in a Christian home never seeing this sort of evangelism in action, I must admit it was admirable and intriguing to see someone carrying the Gospel door to door, just because God said so.

And then he told them, "GO into all the world [every community, every neighborhood, every home (emphasis mine)] and preach the Good News to everyone".

Matthew 16:15 (NLT)

While I was living in rebellion at the time so to speak, I knew of the Lord through what my parents had displayed through their walk with Christ. At that time, however, I was just not ready to make that commitment. Despite the fact I was not ready to commit my life to the Lord, I was not like the other neighbors who looked at Tammie through the peek hole and pretended they were not at home. No, not me. I invited Tammie in each and every time she rang my door bell. She would sometimes sit and talk with me for hours about the goodness of the Lord. Each time our conversations concluded, I told her in no uncertain terms, and with sass, "I'll get saved one day…but it won't be today." Did I mention I would sit proper, legs crossed, with a straight and matter-of-fact face as I said it too? Imagine laboring in conversation for hours, feeling like you are finally breaking through, and then get one of my kind of blows. Well, I smile as I recall Tammie walking away as joyfully as she did when she approached my door each time. She had completed her assignment, and that was enough to satisfy her…and God.

Eventually I was stationed in Korea for a year. My family stayed behind and remained neighbors to Tammie for a while, until she moved. I do not even remember when we exchanged phone numbers, but apparently we had at some point. Upon my return from Korea, I had to go to a military school for a period of time. While at this school, I attended a local church in the area with two sold-out-obedient-to-Christ sisters. Yes, they were all that and then some. Their names are Anjanette, whom I affectionately call Angie; and Martha. Though they could just as easily be nicknamed Apollos, as they were waterers of the seed in their own right. By way of these two ladies I ended up at a church where I received a prophetic word, a word of knowledge that penetrated my heart. Finally, I made that decision to follow Christ. It had been about a year since I had seen or even talked to Tammie. Yet she was one of the first people I called to give the news…that I am now saved and following Christ. Tammie got to hear firsthand that her conversion claim (Me) had been called in.

It was almost twenty years ago when I got to make that phone call to Tammie. Yet I can almost still hear her screaming on the other end of the phone. I remember how she was praising and thanking God for saving my soul. And to this day, what I love the most about her response is she never once made it about her. Tammie, like Paul and Apollos, knew all the glory belonged to God, and she was just happy to partner with Him through her obedience each time he told her to *GO*! Angie and Martha have the same heart concerning the matter. And guess what, I am still in covenant relationship with all of them. As a matter of fact, I can hardly wait for you to read the next segment of this book, *Blessing #7, Boomerang Blessings*, which features another exciting story about a recent encounter with Tammie, more of what God did over her response to His instruction to *GO*!

BLESSINGS #7
BOOMERANG BLESSINGS

As Jesus made his way to Jerusalem, he went along the border between Samaria and Galilee. He was going into a village when he was met by ten men suffering from a dreaded skin disease. They stood at a distance and shouted, "Jesus! Master! Have pity on us!" Jesus saw them and said to them, "Go and let the priests examine you." On the way they were made clean. When one of them saw that he was healed, he came back, praising God in a loud voice. He threw himself to the ground at Jesus' feet and thanked him. The man was a Samaritan. Jesus spoke up, "There were ten who were healed; where are the other nine? Why is this foreigner the only one who came back to give thanks to God?" And Jesus said to him, "Get up and go; your faith has made you well."

Luke 17:11-19 (GNT)

Ever get tired of it seeming like you're the one always pouring out, but no one ever pours back into you? Yet you know you have to just keep doing what God has called you to do. You have to keep going where He sends you. You have to keep speaking what he tells you to speak. If you are absolutely honest, most times you plain out do not even feel like following through with His promptings. You may even be fed up with promises that your season is coming, and "your breakthrough is upon you" type of prophecies. You have heard them so much and for so long that it's almost like white noise each time another prophecy comes.

When Jesus pronounced healing over the ten lepers, he really had no expectations of them. He was just being about the Father's business. Surely it blessed him when the one came back to thank him. And He was even more moved by the fact that out of all those who were healed, it was the foreigner, the Samaritan, who made his way back to bless Jesus by expressing his gratitude for what He had done for him. Now that is just the way it works in the life of the Believer who walks in relentless obedience to God. From whom you least expect, when you least expect it, blessings will come back to you boomerang style.

Blessing #6, Call In Conversion Claims records the story of how my friend and covenant sister, Tammie, led me, and no doubt many others, to the Lord through her obedience. She was committed to her evangelism assignments no matter what. I personally saw her approach the doors of others and walk away when they did not answer. Even I knew they were inside, as most times I saw them return from work, and their vehicles were in their personal parking spaces. The remarkable thing to see was Tammie's joyous smile on her face, despite the outcome. It did not matter that she was indirectly snubbed when the neighbors did not answer the door on purpose. She just kept moving from door to door to door…until she got to mine.

Now I have no idea whether I am the only one who finally opened the door in my complex. I just know when the Lord finally gripped my heart, I was so grateful for the seeds Tammie had planted in it. Over time, through the years, across duty stations I traveled to, etc. I maintained contact with Tammie. It was exciting to tell her the great things God was doing in my life. Our connection quickly grew from witnesser to witnessee…discipler to disciple…eventually evolving into a friendship and sisterhood that still stands strong to this day. Tammie remained an integral part of my journey with the Lord. She got to see me grow in the things of God. I have even been invited to minister to the women's ministry at Tammie's church.

Oftentimes Tammie and I would long to talk to each other over the years. But it was as though God sort of had these boundaries. When we just felt like chit chatting or catching up, we never could make contact with each other. When we finally speak, God always uses one or both of us to give a prophetic word. Mostly it was Tammie giving a word to me. Many of those words are unfolding now. And I marvel at what God is doing in my life, even enabling me to write this book to not only tell stories, but also to give the charge to many who will read it that now is the time to heed the word of the Lord to *GO*! Now is the time to walk in total obedience to Him.

Just a few months ago, I was at home, having taken sick leave for the day. Otherwise I would not have been able to take a phone call. Out of nowhere, Tammie called. During this time, I was facing some major decisions concerning work, ministry, and a potential move in the future. Tammie's timing could not be more perfect, I thought. Surely the Lord knew I needed a prophetic word through a pure voice. And BAM…just like that, a call from my girl Tammie! I began to tell her a bit of what was happening in my world. Then I just began to wait for it…my prophetic word. Tammie started to pray, and yes God began to speak through her…a little. Then the tables turned. Suddenly, the word of the Lord began to flow through me, just like a BOOMERANG, for Tammie!

Because I had not spoken to her in quite some time, I had no idea what was going on in her life, ministry, or world at the time. Nevertheless, the Word of the Lord began to flow through me for Tammie like a river, as though floodgates had been opened up.

Many things she had hidden in her heart, that only her and God knew about. It was the appointed time for Him to breathe life into the dreams and visions He had given her years ago. Yes…when she was pouring into others as God was leading her to do, she did so selflessly, putting her own prophetic promises on hold. And in boomerang fashion, God used me, one of the many she had sown a seed into, to pour back into her. As with the ten lepers, many will get what they need from you, and in some cases even suck the life out of you. But there is always at least one in reserve, who is not just able, but also willing to come back and be a blessing to you too. You just *GO!* You just do as the Lord tells you to. It is inevitable that the blessings will boomerang right back to you.

BLESSING #8
ACCESS TO A FAVOR FEST

And when He was twelve years old, they went up to Jerusalem according to the custom of the feast. When they had finished the days, as they returned, the Boy Jesus lingered behind in Jerusalem. And Joseph and His mother did not know it...Now so it was that after three days they found Him in the temple, sitting in the midst of the teachers, both listening to them and asking them questions...So when they saw Him, they were amazed; and His mother said to Him, "Son, why have You done this to us? Look, Your father and I have sought You anxiously." And He said to them, "Why did you seek Me? Did you not know that I must be about My Father's business?"...Then He went down with them and came to Nazareth, and was subject to them, but His mother kept all these things in her heart. And Jesus increased in wisdom and stature, and in favor with God and men.

Luke 2:42-43; 46; 48-49; 51-52 (NKJV)

A few years ago, I got the opportunity to meet Dr. Dave Martin, who is well-known for his work as a motivational speaker and success coach. Well, I may be using the term "meet" a bit loosely. But I did shake his hand and had a bit of a Kodak moment with him. It was more like I was captivated by his ability to articulate such simple principles related to success in such a profound manner. Dr. Martin spoke at my church; and at a special event for leaders was set up for him to go a little deeper. One particular statement he made that night, which is probably totally unrelated to this book topic, struck me like lightning. At the risk of getting further off topic, I will share the quote anyway;

because I can surely sense your curiosity at this point. Or maybe I just like saying it. At any rate, here goes it:

> *"The only time you do not lose is when you invest in yourself!"*
>
> ~Dr. Dave Martin

At least it is a great quote that is shareworthy. Honestly, I think it was exactly what sent me storming over to Dr. Martin's product table immediately after the final session of the evening. Lest you get confused as to why I was so mesmerized by a talk about success, I will explain a bit more. Dr. Martin also has the ability to craftily intertwine God's word with the principles he shared, which made it all the more relevant for me. As I stepped up to "invest" in me, I was completely satisfied with getting my goods and walking away. However, it might have been perceived as rude since everyone else was getting his autograph and taking a picture. I followed suit.

Maybe Dr. Martin wrote the same thing in every book he signed that night; maybe not. But the inscription he wrote in my book blew me away, *"Favor for you NOW...Luke 2:52"*. It was deeply personal to me based on the season I was in at the time, had been in leading up to this very moment, and have entered into since then. And the addition of the Scripture reference was like icing on the cake. I pretty much knew what it said, as I had read it many times before; but I had to go home and read it several times more to grasp what the Lord was pronouncing to me...right NOW! Admittedly, I had read this so many times passively, as though this promise did not necessarily apply to me, but rather was strictly for Jesus. Yet in that moment it was as though the Holy Spirit whispered me a startling reminder that I am made in His image, according to Genesis 1:27. Suddenly, I could embrace the fact that the promise of favor with God and man was not just for Jesus. The revelation was illuminated...that I, too, can and will and do have favor with God as well as with man. Just like Jesus, I only need to be about my Father's business to attain it and to walk in it.

While I am fascinated by all of Luke Chapter 2, the story line in the focal Scripture verses which brings the chapter to a close is rather intriguing. Following the Passover in Jerusalem, the company of people, which included Jesus' natural parents, Joseph and Mary, set out to return to their home. Joseph and Mary assumed Jesus was among the crowd. When they had not physically seen their son within the first day, they began to search for Him. Imagine their surprise when they realized he was left behind. Now imagine their demeanor when they discovered it was not an oversight, but rather Jesus had his own reason for not following the instructions of the group to head out when it was time. As a mother of three biological children, countless bonus children through foster care, and now even grandchildren; I can say it would not have gone well for me to discover that one of them willfully chose not to do what they were told. But in reading Jesus' response to Mary when she scolded him concerning how anxious they were to find him, I am in awe of his audacity, his boldness, his commitment to the Father, at twelve years old. I am provoked to increase my own capacity of obedience.

If I had to be perfectly honest I would tell you my favorite part of verse 52 used to be the part about increasing in favor. Not anymore. I am now more drawn to the very statement that expresses Jesus' mindset concerning what is on the heart of His Father. He flippantly replied to Mary, "…Did you not know that I must be about my Father's business?" That statement to His earthly mother got me to thinking…wonder if I could have gotten away with sass mouthing my mom like that if I threw God into the mix? Hmmmm…Maybe? Maybe not. On a more serious note, Jesus' statement stirred my thought process for sure. Favor, without measure, will come only when I abandon "my" business for that of my Heavenly Father.

Sometimes I miss the mark with this unconsciously. However, for the most part, from the time I surrendered my life to the Lord,

I have always endeavored to follow after Him, His leading, with reckless abandon. Was it easy? Absolutely not! Did it cost me? Yes…dearly! Would I change a thing about my journey? NO WAY! While my walk with the Lord had many, many challenges attached, I never considered any other option. Not once have I ever considered not serving God since I made that life-altering decision to do so. With bumps and bruises and all along the way, I would say definitively that it worked out superbly for me…Just like it did for Jesus. Yep. Over the years, I have walked in God's unexplainable grace and favor. And yes…with noticeable increase as well.

From very early on in my walk with God, I began to practice obedience in giving. As a result, I have been greatly favored in the area of my finances. Yes, I am bringing up that g-word again. As a babe in Christ, I attended revivals and any service where a move of God was promised. Evangelists and other ministers lifted offerings each night, and I gave not even knowing whether their giving revelations would bear any fruit. Actually, they could have been con artists for all I knew. I was not at all concerned about that. I gave as unto God, eager to obey Him. As a result, I have never wanted for anything, even when I was without employment in the middle of marital separation.

You have also read in the opening of this book about how I obeyed God when He said *GO* here or there. I never questioned…and would only pray and believe He would make the way. Most see me travel and wonder how I do it. Sure, I search for a good deal like everyone else. But most times mega favor shows up in the way of free airline tickets, free hotel rooms, free rental cars, and even money for meals over the years. There were times God moved on the hearts of people and told them to sow into my life, and they do. Many times, I have gone to my mailbox and have received unexpected, and even at times unexplained checks. I will never forget receiving a check with a letter that said something like, "Please do not call and inquire about why you have received this pay out." When something like this happens, you know you are in a favor fest. This. Really. Happened! FYI, I consulted my bank about it, before depositing the check into my account. And yes, that check cleared fine from its bank of origin. Caution: This was before the increase in mail scams. But do you want to know my real secret? It is actually pretty simple:

    Seek.
    Hear.
    Listen Intently.
    OBEY.
    ACCESS Granted...to the FAVOR FEST!

BLESSING #9
DIVINE PROTECTION

*When the day came for the heavenly being to appear before the L*ORD*, Satan was there among them. The L*ORD *asked him, "What have you been doing?" Satan answered, "I have been walking here and there, roaming around the earth." "Did you notice my servant Job?" the L*ORD *asked. "There is no one on earth as faithful and good as he is. He worships me and is careful not to do anything evil." Satan replied, "Would Job worship you if he got nothing out of it? You have always protected him and his family and everything he owns. You bless everything he does, and you have given him enough cattle to fill the whole country. But now suppose you take away everything he has—he will curse you to your face!" "All right,"* *the LORD said to Satan, "everything he has is in your power, but you must not hurt Job himself." So Satan left.*

Job 1:6-12 (GNT)

When the day came for the heavenly beings to appear before the LORD again, Satan was there among them. The LORD asked him, "Where have you been?" Satan answered, "I have been walking here and there, roaming around the earth." "Did you notice my servant Job?" the LORD asked. "There is no one on earth as faithful and good as he is. He worships me and is careful not to do anything evil. You persuaded me to let you attack him for no reason at all, but Job is still as faithful as ever." Satan replied, "A person will give up everything in order to stay alive. But now suppose you hurt his body—he will curse you to your face!" So the LORD said to Satan, "All right, he is in your power, but you are not to kill him."

Job 2:1-6 (GNT)

Walking in obedience to God positions the Believer to receive divine protection. It may not seem like it at times, depending on the level of spiritual attacks some face, but God always maintains a shield around His children and keeps the enemy at bay. Satan can only go as far as he is allowed to go when it comes to demonic attacks. Even in the worst of times, as with Job, we must remember that and endeavor to remain focused and stand firm in our allegiance to the Father, knowing that He is ever present with us.

> *So be strong and courageous! Do not be afraid and do not panic before them. For the LORD your God will personally go ahead of you. He will neither fail you nor abandon you.*
>
> **Deuteronomy 31:6 (NLT)**

Oftentimes while under attack, some may make assumptions concerning your lack of faith in, and even faithfulness to, God. Such reactions to spiritual attacks is merely a sign of immaturity. Just think about. The enemy comes for those who are a threat to his kingdom—those who are committed to God's Kingdom. I have personally read many books and studied the lives of many forerunners and giants in the faith who did great things for God. They all suffered many afflictions. All good soldiers of Jesus Christ will endure hardness—adversity, affliction, discomfort, distress, even death threats (See 2 Timothy 2:3).

Just a couple of months ago, I had my own Job-like encounter in which the enemy literally tried to take me out. On this side of that mega warfare, I now realize he never stood a chance. Satan was limited in what He could do to me. And while it seemed he would succeed, divine protection was on my side through each and every trial, every step of the way. It is safe to say I would never want to repeat what could easily be labeled as a near death experience.

However, I have no regrets about it, and now have a greater understanding of God's ability and willingness to protect me from dangers seen and unseen. He will protect you too!

Prior to Satan's major attack on my life, I started the summer with a bit of pouncing from the enemy, that heightened my awareness of the apparent spiritual warfare taking place. I later learned Satan wanted to stop me from going on certain trips. He knew God had specific assignments for me in each place. And even worse for him, he knew I would obey whatever the assignment the Lord would place before me.

One particular trip was to San Antonio, TX to attend a conference titled UPGRADE, hosted by Apostle Ryan LeStrange. When the conference dates were announced, I was already scheduled to go to Fiji for another event. The flight for Fiji was leaving just one day into UPGRADE. Yet somehow, I sensed I needed to make a sacrifice and get there to attend as much of that conference as possible. I made my travel arrangements accordingly, and flew out of my way from Seattle to San

Antonio, and then on to Los Angeles, where I would travel on to Fiji.

Ironically, when I arrived in San Antonio, I started having some minor health issues. It seemed sinus related. My symptoms were more annoying than anything. I just pressed on and enjoyed what God was doing. Based on what I was experiencing, it was quickly confirmed I had to get to that conference. Then came the flood of nonsensical schemes from the enemy. My daughter had gone into the hospital for an extended stay just before I left home. This is fairly routine since she has cystic fibrosis, except that her lung function was rather low. However, we were confident she would be fine and would have good improvement by the end of her hospitalization, which she did. To complicate matters more for me though was receiving a rather distressing call from my son. He had been rushed to the hospital, and was about to undergo emergency surgery.

WAIT! WHAT?!

Imagine being in another state, headed to another country with not one, but suddenly two children in the hospital. It is of no consequence that they are adults. My children mean the world to me; and I had trouble grasping the fact that I was not there present with them, with all of what was going on. First, I was a complete wreck at the onset of receiving the news. Then I began to pray, and enlisted a few other intercessors to pray as well. At the same time, I was consulting the Lord, I must admit I was planning to cancel going to Fiji. I was prepared to lose all of what I invested to get to my children…until the Holy Spirit intervened and began to break a few things down to me. Here is what I remember from our little conversation that evening, or at least His side of it: "Warfare will not only continue to come; it will intensify. But I will walk you through it every time. You have to keep moving. You have to get to Fiji!"

Holy Spirit speaks to me in many ways; and I welcome whatever form, especially audibly. And this is one of those rare times I felt I could hear those words being spoken directly to me...and in a rather piercing manner. Instantly, I dismissed the thought of turning back and going home. I was determined to get to Fiji by any means necessary, and was open to whatever God's assignment would be for me in that nation. As for my children, my daughter was fine. When she was released from the hospital, her lung function had more than doubled. In the span of her lifetime, having many hospitalizations over the years, I cannot remember her ever having that great of an advancement in such a short span of time. Now the outcome with my son is the true miracle. Talk about divine protection. Each time I talked to him, there was improvement. He was downgraded from needing surgery to a procedure that was not invasive at all. Then it turned out that he did not really need that procedure either, as the infection previously seen had mysteriously left his body. He was released from the hospital within twenty-four hours with no symptoms. Another case of divine protection!

When I drove away from the final session I was able to attend at the UPGRADE Conference, I knew I had fully received all God sent me there for. I was so excited as I boarded the plane in route to LAX, where I would fly to Fiji. Well, my excitement was short lived. Just as I was boarding the plane, still walking down the aisle to my seat, I got a phone call that shocked me to my core. Oh yeah, Satan had pulled out the big guns in another attempt to stop me from going on that trip. The abbreviated version is that my son (while he was still laying up in the hospital) had just been falsely accused of rape.

WHAT ON EARTH?!

Due to the delicacy of the matter attached to this false claim, I will limit the amount of details I share. I will, however, say that it was a last-ditch effort for someone to control the outcome in a matter in which God was (and still is) giving my son great favor. Or better yet, based on the timing, I would say the enemy thought surely this would send me running home right away…instead of continuing on to

Fiji. Lying devil was wrong…AGAIN! Instead, I was more enraged with the enemy after this stunt. When I arrived at the LAX airport, I had only eight hours to work with. I used it to collect myself, console and pray down the power of heaven for my son, and had a conference call with his attorney to strategize concerning what he would face in three days. Outcome: God gave my son victory in that court room! Yep…while I was about my Father's business, divine protection was covering my offspring too. And by the end of my time in Fiji, God had used me to tear down strongholds and prophesy to some of the nation's leaders. That is the abbreviated version of what God did. In short, it was evident to me that I did indeed have to *GO* to Fiji!

Upon my return home, I went into immediate preparation for a mini vacation I had planned for my daughters and me. We were leaving in just four days. We were off to visit a friend in California, as we had done the last few years. We were looking forward to the four days we would be away, and had planned out great fun. Despite the fact I was suddenly not feeling the best, the kids' excitement was enough for me. When we arrived in Sacramento, I felt awful. It appeared I was just dealing with the onset of a minor sinus infection, something I have dealt with before. I had a game plan of hydrating myself and pushing through it. That plan quickly unraveled, as my symptoms became so severe I ended up in the emergency room (ER) in the middle of the night.

No big deal I thought. I was certain I would feel better once I took the prescribed medication. Then I got back to my friend's house, and tried to lay down since I had been up most of the night. Suddenly my son called with horrible news. My dog had gone missing while in his care. If that was not enough, I barely got us both calmed down before my phone rang again. This time it was an investigator from child protective services wanting to interview me. One of my bonus children (a teenager I had in foster care who ran away) had made a false allegation that she got injured in an altercation with me before she left my home. Under any other circumstance (like if I was not so sick with a missing pup), I might find this lie completely hilarious, thinking, "AM I BEING PUNKED?" Nevertheless, when this happened, I knew I was dealing with MEGA WARFARE!

By the end of my four-day trip, I had visited the ER in California three times. By the time I landed back in Seattle, my symptoms had exacerbated. My children had to take me directly to Tacoma General Hospital's ER. Sadly, the physician on duty did not take me seriously. He released me with some written prescriptions, without thoroughly examining me or even considering all of the medications I had received at the three hospital visits prior to this one. Feeling no better than I did when I first arrived at Tacoma General, my son pushed me out in a wheel chair, helped me into his car, and took me home. I was leery about adding more medication to all I had been given over the last few days. Yet I was desperate and not feeling any better. My team of intercessors was praying. I had reached out to other prayer warriors as well. My symptoms continued getting worse. I was in so much pain I could not function, could barely open my eyes, and could barely even talk.

Eventually I dragged myself to the local Rite Aid with the prescription I had received the day before. It was for OxyCotin. I was not familiar with this particular drug, and did not know it was a heavy pain medication. Nothing else had worked for me; and I was naively hopeful this would finally bring me some relief. After taking one pill, I laid down. When I woke up about an hour to an hour and a half later, I felt like something was not right. I had my daughter to call the leader of my intercessory prayer team (Tasha), who is also my spiritual daughter, and who also lives nearby.

We had to make quick decisions, as my symptoms were getting worse. At the time, I had no idea I was having an allergic reaction to the OxyCotin. The ambulance came and did get me to the hospital. Immediately upon arrival, the physician on duty took one look at me and said, "We need to intubate you. Can we intubate you?" Whoa! My mouth and throat were so swollen, they had to put in a breathing tube right away. Allow me to be transparent, at the risk of seeming ignorant, for just a moment. I had no idea what intubation meant when the doctor mentioned the procedure. Do not judge me, as my youngest is the pre-med major, not me. Send me a shout out if you were clueless when you read it at first too. Then I will know we are in the in crowd. At any rate, from that point, I only remember waking up in Good Samaritan Hospital's Intensive Care Unit, where I had laid unconscious for five whole days.

The next twenty-four hours my son filled me in on the happenings of my life during the time I was fully sedated. He explained how the doctors contemplated cutting my throat to do a tracheotomy. Thankfully, Tasha and my son stood firm all week against the doctors' recommendation to do this procedure. When I heard the stories of how persistent they were about it, it was evident to me that the enemy was after my voice, my sound. Since he had failed at keeping me still, he wanted to silence me. Satan was fed up with my persistence and tenacity to obey God at all cost. When he realized he had no power to take me out, his next best shot was to try to shut me up. And even that failed miserably.

WHY?

There is only one logical answer to that question. Even while faced with great adversity, I had done all God required of me. Therefore, I was covered with *DIVINE PROTECTION*…just like Job! Guess what? When you hearken to every time He says *GO*, divine protection is your portion too!

Yolanda Perry

BLESSING #10
ONE OF THEM

[Besides this evidence] it was also established and plainly endorsed by God, Who showed His approval of it by signs and wonders and various miraculous manifestations of [His] power and by imparting the gifts of the Holy Spirit [to the believers] according to His own will.

Hebrews 2:4 (AMP)

Many are feeling wooed to *GO* forth and to carry God's glory from place to place. Some feel like they have a "great" call on their lives, as though it only applies to a select few. Truth is, we are all called to make an impact in the Kingdom of God. Some are called to do so in their local regions; while others are called to the nations. Some are called to the marketplace, while others are called to the church. We must not covet the call of others, but rather be open to *GO* wherever the Father sends us. The most important thing is that we each know exactly where we are called to and are willing fulfill the assignment upon our lives. Also, there are times when God will only release his instructions in bite-sized pieces instead of revealing the fullness of His vision for us. In those times, we have to steward well what He shows us before He begins to release expansion upon our lives.

As I mentioned in one of the earlier stories, the person who witnessed to me went door to door in our little complex as an act of obedience. In her heart, she still carries the vision that God has shown her to *GO* to the nations. I personally have no doubt she will. As a matter of fact, in a sense she has already begun through the seed she has sown in me and the places God is now taking me to. Every *GO* I hearken unto is attached to the deposit and investment she made in me. And every miracle

I experience through my ministry is attached to every *GO* I follow as well.

One such instance of signs and wonders took place earlier this year in the nation of Belize. I remember learning of this particular ministry trip. I really did not even have any idea what it entailed. I just sensed the Lord was beckoning me to *GO*. Now there were several chips stacked against me, one being a barrier with my job. I work as a high school registrar. My position is a one-person operation. It is not even the norm to bring in a substitute when I am out on sick leave. It always operated such that I just catch up whenever I returned to work. As such, due to the nature of my position, it is not customary to ask for time off during the school year, except if an extreme emergency or loss of a loved on occurred. Belize was happening in March, just on the heels of graduation planning, which is also my responsibility.

Ordinarily I would automatically decide I could not *GO* on the trip based on its scheduled timing. Yet I could not shake the thought that I was supposed to. I began to strategize ways in which I could make this work before I went into my boss and asked permission. To my surprise, he was onboard with no hesitations. He even began to give me suggestions on how to do it such that my time off would be minimized. Still in shock, I began to make preparations. Still I had no idea what I was in for during this trip. Honestly, I thought I was just going to support the team and learn as a spectator. Imagine my surprise when I discovered there was an informal preaching schedule being formulated, and I, like everyone else on the trip, would be one of the preachers.

No, I did not completely unravel inside… only halfway is all. Eventually I collected myself and trusted the word of the Lord that was deposited into my spirit for the nation of Belize. I had prayed it through and just needed to release it. I made that sound much easier than it actually was. Nonetheless, I pressed through. I had never used a translator before. I had never preached internationally before. I had never ministered with this group before. I had never received a word like this before. However, I have served my God, who is all-knowing; and this was not His first rodeo. Further, I have always known Him to come through for me every single time.

When God gave me the word for Belize, it was somewhat unusual. It was not a common word to me, and certainly not one I use in everyday conversation. To top it off, He only gave me one word, "DOWNPOUR". I remember pondering it for a few days, hoping to develop a message from it. There seemed to be a blockage. Then I realized it was not a mere message, but a prophetic word God was preparing for the nation and that the one word was simply going to be a springboard. The day I was scheduled to preach, I was already feeling a bit nervous and feeling a little intimidated by all of what had taken place through ministry the days leading up to this moment. To heighten my anxiety, a bit of a shift took place when suddenly it was decided my spiritual father would preach for a few moments before I got up. My first thought was, "Oh no…me go after him?!" If you have ever heard or seen Apostle Ryan LeStrange minister, you would understand why I would be shaking in my boots. Actually, it was hot out. So, I might have actually been wearing flip flops that night, but shivering nonetheless.

In the moments that led up to me releasing the word, I had to remind myself that God was in control. Further, this was His show, His production. It certainly was not a Last Preacher Standing competition. And I needed to get past me so God could speak through me to His people. Surely the people were hungry and thirsty for more. As I began, God instructed me to sing over them and encourage them that it was a new season for Belize. Then I began to share from the Word, gleaning from the story about the end of the drought in 1 Kings, Chapter 18.

> *Elijah said to Ahab, "Go up, eat and drink, for there is the sound of a rainstorm." So Ahab went to eat and drink, but Elijah went up to the summit of Carmel. He bowed down on the*

ground and put his face between his knees. Then he said to his servant, "Go up and look toward the sea." So he went up, looked, and said, "There's nothing." Seven times Elijah said, "Go back." On the seventh time, he reported, "There's a cloud as small as a man's hand coming from the sea." Then Elijah said, "Go and tell Ahab, 'Get your chariot ready and go down so the rain doesn't stop you.'" In a little while, the sky grew dark with clouds and wind, and there was a downpour. So Ahab got in his chariot and went to Jezreel.

1 Kings 18:41-45 (HCSB)

I remember sensing that the people of Belize were experiencing a spiritual drought, and God had sent our team to encourage them, to quench their thirst. Much had already taken place in all the churches we visited that week, but this night I felt like God was going to go above and beyond with demonstration. He certainly did. After I preached, the entire team helped praying for the people, many were touched, filled and some refilled with the Holy Spirit. Many were slain in the Spirit while others broke out into holy laughter. God had surely poured out in that place. Yet He was not through.

That night God was intent on proving how real He is to the people in Belize. Once everyone got settled after I had preached, there was one last speaker of the evening. Just as he mounted the platform and got started, we heard a pounding noise coming from the ceiling. Out of nowhere it started to rain heavily. More accurately, it started to DOWNPOUR. When everyone realized God was confirming His word with signs and wonders following, there was a sudden breakout of people dancing. You bet I was in that number too.

Following that moment, I began to ponder how one act of obedience, heeding God's instruction to *GO* to Belize, resulted in an experience that would permanently mark my ministry. To this day I am encouraged when my spiritual father calls me *The Rainmaker*. That moment fueled my faith all the more concerning other promises God has made to me about other signs that would occur in my ministry. Even as I close this chapter, I am reminded of the Scripture that speaks of signs following those who believe:

> *And these signs will follow those who believe: In My name they will cast out demons; they will speak with new tongues; they will take up serpents; and if they drink anything deadly, it will by no means hurt them; they will lay hands on the sick, and they will recover."*
>
> **Mark 16:17-18 (NKJV)**

Well, I believe. So I must be one of "them"…the "them" spoken of in this verse. When I *GO* forth in faith, believing the One who has called me, who is sending me, surely the signs will follow. I am not sure about you, but I am sick and tired of being a spectator, hearing about and watching God do miracles through others. I am no longer satisfied reading about what He did through miracle gurus like

Smith Wigglesworth, Kathryn Kuhlman, Aimee Simple McPherson and many other pioneers of the faith. I am convinced not only could He do it through them, but through my obedience, I am blessed to be ONE OF THEM...and so are you! No more excuses. No more sitting on the sidelines. It is time that we get in agreement with and alignment with His Word...and do the greater works that Jesus prophesied we would do.

> *I tell you the truth, anyone who believes in me will do the same works I have done, and even greater works, because I am going to be with the Father.*
>
> **John 12:12 (NLT)**

Ready. Set. ***GO!***

CONCLUSION

When Abram was ninety-nine years old, the LORD appeared to him and said, "I am El-Shaddai—'God Almighty.' Serve me faithfully and live a blameless life. I will make a covenant with you, by which I will guarantee to give you countless descendants." At this, Abram fell face down on the ground. Then God said to him, "This is my covenant with you: I will make you the father of a multitude of nations! What's more, I am changing your name. It will no longer be Abram. Instead, you will be called Abraham, for you will be the father of many nations. I will make you extremely fruitful. Your descendants will become many nations, and kings will be among them!

Genesis 17:1-6 (NLT)

Then God said to Abraham, "Regarding Sarai, your wife—her name will no longer be Sarai. From now on her name will be Sarah. And I will bless her and give you a son from her! Yes, I will bless her richly, and she will become the mother of many nations. Kings of nations will be among her descendants."

Genesis 17:15-16 (NLT)

I reckon Abram did not fully grasp all that was in store for him when he set out to obey God. He went in faith, relying on God to lead, guide and direct him along the way. And He did. It was not overnight, but God kept His promise to Abram that He would make his name great. Here in the above scriptures, we see God's promise to Abram unfolding in that He renamed him Abraham, to match the blessings He was about to bestow upon him. Surely Abraham was beyond grateful to just receive what God was doing in his life. But we serve a God who does not stop at fulfilling a promise. He goes above and beyond. When He upgraded Abram's life (to Abraham, father of many nations), He decided to do the same for his wife. He changed Sarai's name as well…to Sarah, in keeping with her calling as the mother of many nations.

God is pouring out the same measure of blessings today, to those who are willing to walk in that same level of obedience; to those who are willing to *GO* when He says *GO*, with no questions asked. So far you have read about ten blessings that follow when we obey His still small voice. This list is not, by any means, exhaustive. The blessings of the Lord are endless. They will continue to flow as long as we continue to walk upright before Him, hearken unto His promptings, and take heed when He speaks.

What is that we hear Him saying?

GO! GO! GO!

EPILOGUE

Just weeks prior to receiving the charge to write this book, I was on the Belize trip I spoke of in *Blessing #10, One of Them*. The whole experience was prophetic and surreal all at the same time; but I sensed God doing something profound in my life. I sensed major transition ahead, which usually would cause me to feel a little anxious. However, I was at peace with what I was sensing. While our teams were on a mission to prophesy over the land, I received a message from my dear friend, Kelly Balarie. She had a dream she knew she had to share with me. Kelly's timing could not have been more spot on. She had no idea I was out of the country for ministry or how God was dealing with me in that moment. When I received the charge to write this book, her words came flooding back to my memory. It is not the norm for me to share private messages. But this exchange fits so well with the message of *GO!* I sense it is a NOW word to the Body of Christ in this hour. The end of my correspondence with Kelly gives a prophetic charge. I felt I needed to share it with you. I hope it provokes you just like it did me. I will close with the contents of our conversation:

> ***KELLY:*** *Last night I had this awesome dream of God moving the heavens to make things happen. His Kingdom was in motion. I don't know if this has ever happened to you, but I had a deep and tangible understanding that he was moving powerful things. In my dream, I asked him who this was for – he said you! Woot! Woot! GO Yolanda. The kingdom was shifting in support of you and his heart is moving for you. I woke up in complete praise!*
>
> ***ME****: Whoa!!! This (praise) is what came out when I read that. I am in Belize for ministry and literally thought of you just yesterday. I'm speechless and FLOORED! Oh my...*

KELLY: *I asked him in the dream, "Who? He said you. I felt the heavens moving for you. I knew that something was shifting. Excited to hear what happens...I am praying for you. I know I am repeating things, but it was powerful!*

ME: *Keep it coming! You have no idea what this means...such confirmation!*

KELLY: *Thank you God. I am so glad. I rejoice with you. I praise God that he is at work. I am thankful to be his messenger. I cheer you on. I applaud his great power to move heaven and earth. I am eager to hear his great unfolding under your feet. All for his name, all for his glory...be expectant and steadfast. Stay close to his heart.*

Take risk. Step in. GO.

BIBLE VERSION KEY

AMP	Amplified Bible
BSB	Berean Study Bible
CEV	Contemporary English Version
ESV	English Standard Version
GNT	Good News Translation
GW	GOD'S WORD Translation
HCSB	Holman Christian Standard Bible
KJV	King James Version
MSG	The Message
NASB	New American Standard Bible
NIV	New International Version
NKJV	New King James Version
NLT	New Living Translation
TLB	The Living Bible

ABOUT THE AUTHOR

Yolanda Perry is an emerging prophetic voice in the hour. She is the author of *Worth the Wait*, which she released in 2007. Yolanda has served in all facets of ministry, to include leading women's ministry at her local church for five years; also ministering at the Washington State Corrections Center for Women for over ten years, where she led hundreds to salvation and witnessed many lives being transformed.

Yolanda served 11 years in the US Army. She holds academic degrees in concentrations, such as Business Administration, Education, and Ministry & Church Leadership. But she is most proud to be a continual student of School of the Holy Spirit.

Currently Yolanda serves as part of the prayer team at Eastpointe Church in Puyallup, WA. She is aligned with TRIBE Network under the leadership of Apostle Ryan LeStrange. Yolanda also serves as the lead intercessor of RLM Prayer Shield.

As a gifted speaker and writer, Yolanda's personal mission is to communicate and demonstrate unshakable faith. She currently writes inspirational messages and blogs on her Facebook page and website, www.speak2myheart.org. She has been privileged to travel nationally and internationally carrying the Gospel of Jesus Christ, fulfilling God's mandate that she would go to the nations.

Now that Yolanda has fully embraced the charge to *GO*, you will see and hear much of her through her writings in books, audio and live messages, and throughout all social media outlets.

Yolanda is the proud mother of three biological children, countless bonus kids through foster care, and is a beloved Nonnie to her beautiful grandkids.